Pet Care and Training

Paw-sitive Pet Care

Hina Victor

Dedication

In this genuine aide, we leave on an excursion of commitment to our darling fuzzy mates. Pets give pleasure, genuine love, and friendship into our lives, improving us people with each sway of a tail or delicate murmur. This book fills in as a recognition for the bond we share with our pets and as a far reaching asset to assist us with becoming dependable, mindful, and learned pet guardians.

Together, we should investigate the domains of pet consideration and preparing, sustaining our pets' prosperity and improving their lives.

Part 1: Embracing the Job of a Pet Parent

The Delight of Pet Friendship: Grasping the significant effect of pets in our lives.

Obligations and Responsibility: Setting ourselves up for a long period of really focusing on our creature companions.

Picking the Right Pet: Investigating different pet species and tracking down the ideal counterpart for our way of life and inclinations.

Part 2: The Groundworks of Pet Consideration

Sustenance and Taking care of Rules: Giving a decent and healthy eating regimen for our pets.

Prepping Basics: Keeping up with cleanliness and keeping our pets looking and feeling their best.

Establishing a Protected Climate: Pet-sealing our homes and guaranteeing a solid residing space.

Part 3: Wellbeing and Health

Deterrent Consideration: The significance of normal veterinary check-ups and inoculations.

Indications of Ailment: Perceiving normal medical problems and looking for brief clinical consideration.

Mental and Actual Activity: Animating our pets' psyches and bodies for generally prosperity.

Part 4: Encouraging feedback Preparing

The Force of Positive Preparation: Embracing reward-based strategies for powerful learning.

Fundamental Acquiescence Orders: Showing fundamental orders like sit, remain, and review.

Tending to Social Difficulties: Answers for normal issues like yelping, biting, and digging.

Part 5: Preparing for Unique Abilities

High level Preparation: Investigating stunts, deftness, and aroma discovery exercises to challenge our pets.
Treatment and Administration Creature Preparing: Understanding what our pets can make a positive mean for locally.
Everyday encouragement Preparing: Sustaining close to home bonds and giving help to our pets as a trade off.
Part 6: Improving Your Pet's Life

Holding and Correspondence: Fortifying the close to home association with our pets.
Recess and Toys: The meaning of play in keeping our pets blissful and locked in.
Do-It-Yourself Pet Tasks: Making fun and intuitive toys and exercises for our fuzzy companions.
End:
As we finish up our excursion of commitment to pet consideration and preparing, let us invest heavily in the development and satisfaction we bring to our pets' lives. Keep in mind, being a dependable pet parent is a continuous responsibility loaded up with adoration, tolerance, and understanding. Through this devotion, we can fashion a solid bond that endures forever, making treasured recollections with our darling pets. Together, how about we commend the delight and satisfaction of pet possession, imparting our lives to these striking creatures who improve our reality in endless ways.

Hina Victor

Table of Contents

Foreword

As I pen down these words for the foreword of "Pet Consideration and Preparing," I'm loaded up with enormous appreciation and fervor. This book isn't simply one more aide; a close to home excursion praises the significant association among people and their valued creature mates.

Our affection for pets exceeds all rational limitations. They show us significant life illustrations: reliability, absolution, and genuine love. Their presence acquires comfort seasons of pain and bliss in snapshots of win. Consequently, it is our obligation as pet guardians to give them the most ideal consideration and supporting.

"Pet Consideration and Preparing" is a mother lode of information and knowledge, mindfully organized to take care of both beginner pet people and prepared fans. Whether you have recently invited another fuzzy companion into your life or have imparted endless recollections to your darling pets, this book is a significant asset to direct you on the way of capable pet proprietorship.

The excursion to turning into a dependable and empathetic pet parent begins with figuring out the major necessities of our creature companions. From giving legitimate sustenance and prepping to establishing a protected and invigorating climate, every perspective is fundamental for their prosperity.

Preparing is one more essential part of our pets' lives, deeply shaping their way of behaving and upgrading the bond we share. The book dives into uplifting feedback techniques, displaying how tolerance and consolation can change our pets into polite, cheerful friends.

Past the viable perspectives, "Pet Consideration and Preparing" dives into the profound parts of pet possession. The adoration we share with our pets is unrestricted, and this book underscores the significance of holding, correspondence, and everyday encouragement. Together, we can give a supporting and satisfying life for our pets, enhancing their lives as they improve our own.

I compliment the creator for their commitment and mastery in making this outstanding aide. It is obvious that they share similar energy for pets as we do, and their insight radiates through the pages of this book. I'm certain that "Pet Consideration and Preparing" will turn into a vital ally to pet guardians around the world, encouraging a local area of mindful, mindful, and informed parental figures.

To every one of the peruses setting out on this excursion, may you track down motivation and insight inside these pages. Embrace the delight and obligation that accompany pet possession, and appreciate the interesting bond you share with your fuzzy colleagues. Together, let us commend the magnificence of this relationship and make an existence where pets are cherished, really focused on, and appreciated as treasured individuals from our families.

Hina Victor

Preface

Welcome to "Pet Consideration and Preparing," a complete aide committed to encouraging a profound and cherishing association among you and your dearest creature mates. As an eager pet sweetheart and fan, I'm excited to impart this sincere excursion to you, pointed toward giving the information and devices important to turn into a dependable, merciful, and educated pet parent.

All through my life, I have encountered the delight and satisfaction that comes from offering my home to pets. Each sway of a tail, delicate murmur, or happy hello has enhanced my life in manners that words can scarcely portray. This book is a demonstration of the significant effect that our pets have on our prosperity, showing us fundamental ethics like compassion, persistence, and the magnificence of straightforward joys.

The motivation behind "Pet Consideration and Preparing" originates from my longing to make an asset that takes care of the different necessities of pet people and forthcoming pet guardians the same. Whether you are inviting another fuzzy companion into your home or looking to reinforce your bond with a long-lasting buddy, this guide is customized to give pragmatic counsel and master experiences to improve your pet nurturing venture.

To a limited extent 1 of this book, we dig into the essentials of pet consideration. Understanding the exceptional prerequisites of each pet species is essential to guaranteeing their physical and profound prosperity. From picking the right pet for your way of life to establishing a supporting climate and carrying out legitimate nourishment and prepping rehearses, you will track down an abundance of data to address your pet's issues.

Section 2 is devoted to uplifting feedback preparing methods. We investigate how love, persistence, and grasping structure the underpinning of viable preparation. Through these techniques, you can fabricate areas of strength for a believing relationship with your pet, empowering appropriate conduct and tending to any difficulties that might emerge.

Past the reasonable angles, Section 3 dives into the profound elements of pet proprietorship. Our pets are something other than creatures; they are relatives, associates, and wellsprings of unfathomable love. Figuring out how to speak with them, offer close to home help, and support their prosperity is similarly fundamental for their joy and yours.

I should offer my genuine thanks to the specialists and individual pet darlings who contributed their insight and encounters to enhance this book. Their significant experiences and enthusiasm for creature government assistance have raised "Pet Consideration and Preparing" to a really comprehensive aide.

As we set out on this excursion together, I urge you to move toward pet consideration and preparing with an open heart and an eagerness to learn and develop. May this book act as a reference point of information, directing you to turn into the best pet parent you can be, and producing an enduring and esteemed bond with your shaggy buddy.

Much thanks to you for picking "Pet Consideration and Preparing" as your sidekick on this exceptional excursion. Allow us to praise the delight, love, and giggling that our pets bring into our lives, as we endeavor to give them enough best consideration and the hottest hug.

Hina Victor

Introduction

Welcome to "Pet Consideration and Preparing," an exhaustive aide intended to improve the existences of both pet people and their cherished creature sidekicks. Whether you have quite recently invited another fuzzy companion into your home or have imparted endless recollections to your devoted pets, this book is your go-to asset for giving the most ideal consideration and supporting for your four-legged relatives.

The connection among people and creatures is really extraordinary. Our pets offer us genuine love, steadfast faithfulness, and a remarkable feeling of satisfaction that lights up even our most obscure days. As capable pet guardians, it is our honor and obligation to respond that affection by guaranteeing their prosperity and satisfaction.

The excursion of pet possession is both fulfilling and satisfying, yet it additionally accompanies its difficulties and vulnerabilities. From choosing the right pet for your way of life to understanding their extraordinary requirements, each step of this excursion is pivotal to building an agreeable and deep rooted relationship with your fuzzy buddy.

"Pet Consideration and Preparing" isn't simply an aide; it is a genuine investigation of the numerous features of pet possession. Inside these pages, you will track down commonsense exhortation, master tips, and endearing stories that outline the significant effect pets have on our lives and how, thus, we can make a positive effect in theirs.

In the principal segment of this book, we plunge into the essentials of pet consideration. Understanding your pet's species-explicit necessities is fundamental to furnishing them with a solid and blissful life. We investigate subjects like sustenance, preparing, work out, and establishing a protected climate that encourages their physical and close to home prosperity.

The subsequent segment is given to encouraging feedback preparing procedures. Preparing isn't just about showing your pet fundamental orders; it is a potential chance to fabricate serious areas of strength for an in view of trust, regard, and correspondence. You will find viable preparation strategies that stress tolerance, consideration, and consistency, assisting you with sustaining a polite and certain pet.

In the third and last area, we dive into the close to home parts of pet possession. Our pets are aware creatures with feelings and requirements, very much like us. Grasping their language and offering close to home help are significant to establishing a cherishing and improving climate that advances their bliss and mental prosperity.

All through this excursion, you will find stories and tales shared by individual pet darlings, every one a demonstration of the extraordinary force of the human-creature bond. These genuine encounters offer motivation, consolation, and an update that the difficulties of pet consideration and preparing are shared and conquerable.

As we adventure into this investigation of pet consideration and preparing, I ask you to embrace each second with an open heart and a readiness to learn and develop. May this book act as your directing light, offering experiences, arrangements, and the certainty to be the best pet parent your shaggy companion merits.

Much obliged to you for picking "Pet Consideration and Preparing" as your buddy on this staggering excursion. Together, we should praise the delight, love, and perpetual dedication that our pets bring into our lives as we endeavor to be the pet guardians they gaze upward to and appreciate

Hina Victor

Chapter 1
The Complete Guide to Pet Care and Training

There is a one of a kind satisfaction that comes from imparting our lives to pets. The swaying tails, delicate murmurs, and loving prods advise us that we are in good company in this world. In this initial area, we investigate the significant effect of pet friendship on our physical and profound prosperity. Understanding the prizes that accompany pet proprietorship makes way for a satisfying excursion into the domain of pet consideration and preparing.

1.1 The Human-Creature Bond:
Dive into the science and brain research behind the human-creature bond. Figure out how our pets become something other than creatures; they become esteemed individuals from our families, offering daily encouragement and unrestricted love.

1.2 The Mending Force of Pets:
Find the restorative advantages of pet proprietorship. From decreasing pressure and uneasiness to advancing cardiovascular wellbeing, pets emphatically affect our general prosperity, both intellectually and truly.

1.3 Picking the Right Pet:
Prior to setting out on the excursion of pet consideration and preparing, finding the ideal counterpart for your way of life and day to day environment is fundamental. Investigate different pet species, their requirements, and the obligations that accompany every decision.

Area 2: Obligations and Responsibility

2.1 The Responsibility of Pet Proprietorship:

Possessing a pet is a long lasting responsibility. In this part, we stress the significance of understanding the obligations that accompany really focusing on one more residing being and the commitment expected to give a caring home.

2.2 Monetary Contemplations:
Pets accompany monetary obligations, from normal veterinary visits to giving quality food and toys. Figure out how to spending plan successfully for pet consideration without undermining their prosperity.

2.3 Time and Consideration:
Pets blossom with consideration and friendship. Investigate ways of adjusting your day to day everyday practice and devote time to sustain your pets sincerely and intellectually.

Segment 3: Planning for Pet Being a parent

3.1 Pet-Sealing Your Home:
Establish a protected climate for your new fuzzy companion by distinguishing likely dangers and pet-sealing your living spaces.

3.2 Supplies and Basics:
From food and water dishes to prepping instruments and toys, this segment gives an extensive agenda of fundamental supplies to guarantee your pet's solace and prosperity.

3.3 Acquainting Another Pet with Your Home:
On the off chance that you have existing pets or are presenting a pet interestingly, get familiar with the prescribed procedures for acquainting them with guarantee a smooth and tranquil change.

End:
The principal section of "The Total Manual for Pet Consideration and Preparing" establishes the groundwork for a compensating venture into pet possession. We have investigated the delight of the human-creature bond, the obligations that

accompany really focusing on a pet, and the planning expected to invite another shaggy sidekick into your home. With this information, you are exceptional to leave on the following parts, which dive into the reasonable parts of pet consideration and uplifting feedback preparing procedures. Embrace the difficulties and delights of pet life as a parent, and allow us together to establish a cherishing and satisfying climate for our darling pets.

Chapter 2
Paws and Purr-fection

An even and nutritious eating regimen is the foundation of a solid and cheerful pet. In this part, we dig into the significance of appropriate nourishment and investigate dietary rules for different pet species. Understanding their healthful requirements permits us to give our shaggy companions the fuel they need to flourish.

1.1 Disentangling Pet Sustenance:
Find the key supplements fundamental for your pet's general wellbeing, including proteins, fats, sugars, nutrients, and minerals. Figure out how to peruse pet food names and go with informed decisions for their prosperity.

1.2 Fitting Weight control plans to Pet Species:
Various pets have different dietary prerequisites. Whether you have a canine, feline, bunny, bird, or other little warm blooded creatures, this part gives species-explicit dietary proposals.

1.3 Exceptional Weight control plans for Ailments:
Investigate remedial weight control plans for pets with explicit ailments or dietary awareness's, permitting you to help their general wellbeing and deal with any clinical worries.

Area 2: Preparing and Cleanliness Fundamentals

2.1 The Significance of Normal Preparing:
Preparing is something other than keeping your pet looking clean; it is critical for their skin, coat, and generally solace. Learn appropriate prepping methods and comprehend how preparing reinforces the human-creature bond.

2.2 Washing Your Pet:

Find the craft of washing your pets without causing unjustifiable pressure, making bath time a positive and pleasant experience for both you and your fuzzy companion.

2.3 Nail Managing and Ear Cleaning:
Learn protected and powerful techniques to manage your pet's nails and clean their ears, guaranteeing their general prosperity and forestalling potential medical problems.

Segment 3: Establishing a Protected and Invigorating Climate

3.1 The Significance of Activity:
Standard active work is crucial for your pet's psychological and actual wellbeing. Find different ways of connecting with your pet in play and exercise, custom-made to their species and individual necessities.

3.2 Improvement Exercises:
Investigate innovative and animating exercises to forestall fatigue and advance mental enhancement. From puzzle toys to intelligent play, these exercises keep your pets intellectually sharp and content.

3.3 Guaranteeing Security at Home:
Establish a pet-accommodating home climate by distinguishing likely perils and carrying out security measures to safeguard your shaggy friend from mishaps.

End:
Part 2 of "Paws and Murmur faction" centers on fundamental pet consideration procedures to guarantee your pets carry on with their best lives. We have investigated the meaning of ideal nourishment, legitimate prepping, and an invigorating climate custom fitted to your pet's requirements. By furnishing our pets with the consideration and consideration they merit, we construct areas of strength for a for a long period of joy and prosperity. As we continue on toward the following section, we will dive into the

specialty of encouraging feedback preparing, extending our bond with our pets and sustaining their social turn of events. Together, let us establish a climate of adoration, care, and "murmur faction" for our darling shaggy sidekicks.

Chapter 3
Pet Parenting

In this part, we dig further into the significant and special connection among people and their adored pets. Pet nurturing is something beyond accommodating their actual necessities; it includes sustaining profound associations, figuring out their way of behaving, and establishing an amicable home climate. Allow us to investigate the complexities of pet nurturing and the delights it brings to our lives.

1.1 Close to home Association and Correspondence:
Comprehend how pets speak with us through non-verbal communication, vocalizations, and other unobtrusive prompts. Reinforcing this bond upgrades our capacity to answer their feelings and cultivates common comprehension.

1.2 The Force of Sympathy:
Find the significance of sympathy in pet nurturing. By relating to our pets, we can give them the adoration, care, and backing they need to have a good sense of reassurance and content.

1.3 The Mending Presence of Pets:
Investigate the remedial advantages of having pets, as they offer daily encouragement and solace during testing times, giving a feeling of quiet and prosperity.

Segment 2: Profound Prosperity of Pets

2.1 Perceiving Pressure and Tension:
Figure out how to distinguish indications of stress and tension in your pets, as well as the normal triggers that can disturb their profound equilibrium.

2.2 Giving a Place of refuge:

Establish a solid and encouraging climate for your pets, offering them a retreat where they have a good sense of security and safeguarded.

2.3 Tending to Fearing abandonment:
Find techniques to assist pets with adapting to fearing abandonment, guaranteeing they keep quiet and loose when let be.

Segment 3: Uplifting feedback Preparing

3.1 The Groundwork of Uplifting feedback:
Comprehend the standards of uplifting feedback preparing, underscoring prizes and consolation to build up wanted ways of behaving.

3.2 Preparation Fundamental Orders:
Figure out how to show your pets fundamental orders, for example, sit, remain, come, and heel, utilizing uplifting feedback methods to guarantee a blissful and compensating preparing experience.

3.3 Critical thinking and Changing on a surface level:
Investigate positive strategies to resolve normal conduct issues, like exorbitant yapping, biting, and bouncing, advancing positive conduct changes without depending on discipline.

Segment 4: Supporting the Pet-Parent Relationship

4.1 Quality Time and Holding:
Invest quality energy with your pets, taking part in exercises that fortify your bond and extend your association.

4.2 Activity and Play:
Find the meaning of recess and practice in building serious areas of strength for a with your pets, offering both mental and actual excitement.

4.3 Tuning in and Noticing:

Get familiar with the craft of undivided attention and perception, permitting you to more readily figure out your pets' requirements and feelings.

End:

Section 3 of our pet consideration and preparing guide centers around the profound parts of pet nurturing. By developing a profound bond with our pets, figuring out their feelings, and carrying out encouraging feedback preparing, we establish a climate of affection, trust, and understanding. As pet guardians, we are endowed with the prosperity and bliss of these brilliant creatures who give such a lot of pleasure to our lives. With sympathy, empathy, and devotion, let us sustain a relationship loaded up with adoration and happiness, manufacturing a strong bond with our dearest shaggy friends.

Chapter 4
From Woofs to Whiskers

Canines have been our unwavering allies for quite a long time, while felines have caught our hearts with their strange appeal. In this part, we investigate the one of a kind qualities of canines and felines, giving experiences into their way of behaving, necessities, and how to make a cherishing and satisfying relationship with these darling pets.

1.1 The Canine World:
Dig into the universe of canines, figuring out their pack attitude, social construction, and how they speak with one another and with us.

1.2 Canine Non-verbal communication:
Figure out how to decipher canine non-verbal communication and vocalizations, permitting you to more readily grasp your canine's feelings and requirements.

1.3 Cat Interest:
Find the puzzling universe of felines, appreciating their autonomy, correspondence style, and the meaning of their perplexing ways of behaving.

Area 2: Canine Consideration and Preparing

2.1 Wellbeing and Nourishment for Canines:
Figure out the special dietary necessities of canines, and investigate preventive medical care measures to keep your canine sidekick in ideal wellbeing.

2.2 Fundamental Acquiescence Preparing for Canines:
Get familiar with the basics of encouraging feedback preparing for canines, training them fundamental orders and ways of behaving to turn out to be polite and respectful mates.

2.3 Tending to Social Difficulties in Canines:
Investigate viable and empathetic techniques to oversee and change normal social issues in canines, for example, chain pulling, yapping, and fear of abandonment.

Area 3: Cat Care and Preparing

3.1 Ideal Wellbeing and Nourishment for Felines:
Find the dietary requirements of felines and investigate preventive medical care practices to guarantee your catlike companion carries on with a long and sound life.

3.2 Litter Preparing and Cat Manners:
Figure out how to effectively litter train your feline and address normal cat ways of behaving to keep an amicable home climate.

3.3 Preparation Strategies for Felines:
While felines are free animals, they can likewise be prepared. Investigate encouraging feedback strategies to show your feline new ways of behaving and deceives.

Segment 4: Making an Agreeable Home for Both

4.1 Presenting Canines and Felines:
On the off chance that you have the two canines and felines in your family, gain proficiency with the prescribed procedures for acquainting them with cultivate a quiet concurrence.

4.2 Comprehension and Forestalling Pet Contentions:
Investigate techniques to forestall clashes among canines and felines, advancing a tranquil and agreeable climate for all your fuzzy relatives.

4.3 Sustaining the Connection among Canines and Felines:

Value the delightful fellowships that can shape among canines and felines, and track down ways of cultivating positive cooperation's and associations.

End:

Section 4 of "From Woofs to Bristles" offers an extensive comprehension of the two canines and felines, commending their novel characteristics and qualities. By dominating pet consideration and preparing strategies custom-made to every species, we can construct major areas of strength for a warm security with our shaggy companions. Whether it's a swaying tail or a delicate murmur, let us treasure the delight and unrestricted love our pets bring into our lives, embracing the job of dependable pet guardians for our dearest canines and felines..

Chapter 5
Training Tails and Happy Trails

In this part, we leave on an excursion of uplifting feedback preparing, a humane and compelling way to deal with deeply shaping our pets' way of behaving. By zeroing in on remunerations, support, and shared understanding, we can establish an agreeable and cheerful climate for our fuzzy sidekicks.

1.1 Grasping Uplifting feedback:
Investigate the science behind uplifting feedback preparing and how it advances trust, certainty, and a more grounded connection among pet and proprietor.

1.2 The Job of Remunerations:
Find out about various sorts of remunerations, from treats and toys to acclaim and friendship, and how to utilize them successfully in preparing.

1.3 Structure Trust and Certainty:
Find the meaning of building trust and trust in the preparation cycle, permitting your pet to have a real sense of safety and anxious to learn.

Segment 2: Preparing Fundamental Orders

2.1 Showing Fundamental Dutifulness Orders:
Become amazing at showing basic orders, for example, sit, remain, come, and leave it, furnishing your pet with the devices to effectively explore day to day existence.

2.2 Rope Preparing and Free Chain Strolling:
Figure out how to walk your canine on a free rope, making strolls a pleasant encounter for both you and your canine sidekick.

2.3 Litter Preparing and Review for Felines:

Investigate procedures to prepare your feline to utilize the litter box reliably and how to train them to come when called.

Segment 3: Critical thinking and Changing outwardly

3.1 Tending to Undesirable Ways of behaving:
Find positive techniques to address and alter undesirable ways of behaving in your pet, like hopping, digging, and unreasonable yelping.

3.2 Fear of abandonment and Unfortunate Ways of behaving:
Investigate humane methodologies to assist pets with adapting to fearing abandonment and dread, making a feeling of safety and quiet.

3.3 Counter-Molding and Desensitization:
Figure out how to utilize counter-molding and desensitization procedures to assist pets with defeating fears and fears in a delicate and steady way.

Area 4: High level Preparation Methods

4.1 Stunts and Fun Ways of behaving:
Connect with your pet's brain and innovativeness by showing them fun stunts and ways of behaving, fortifying the connection among you and empowering mental feeling.

4.2 Readiness and Canine Games:
Find the intriguing universe of canine games and readiness preparing, giving physical and mental difficulties to canines of all varieties and sizes.

4.3 Help and Treatment Creature Preparing:
Investigate the extraordinary preparation expected for administration and treatment creatures, understanding what they can make a positive mean for in the existences of others.

End:

Section 5 of "Preparing Tails and Cheerful Paths" commends the excursion of encouraging feedback preparing and the change it brings to our pets' way of behaving and prosperity. By embracing prizes, support, and understanding, we make a preparation experience overflowing with bliss and energy. As we adventure forward with our respectful and satisfied pets, let us keep on sustaining the exceptional bond we share, making a long period of cheerful paths and euphoric experiences together. With affection and commitment, we can enable our pets to be their best selves, fabricating a striking organization in light of trust and concordance.

Chapter 6
The Pet Whisperer

In this part, we dig into the job of a "Pet Whisperer" - a pet parent who speaks with their shaggy friends on a profound and natural level. By understanding creature conduct and non-verbal communication, we can become sensitive to our pets' necessities and feelings, encouraging a significant and compassionate association.

1.1 The Language of Creatures:

Investigate the unpretentious subtleties of creature correspondence, from swaying tails and murmuring to vocalizations and body stances, figuring out how to decipher everything that our pets are saying to us.

1.2 The Force of Compassion in Pet Nurturing:

Grasp the meaning of sympathy in pet nurturing, and how it permits us to see the world through our pets' eyes, cultivating a more profound bond based on understanding and empathy.

1.3 The Association of Energy and Feelings:

Find what our profound energy means for our pets as well as the other way around, establishing an amicable and adjusted climate for both human and creature.

Segment 2: Uplifting feedback Preparing with Heart

2.1 Preparation with Compassion:

Investigate the craft of preparing your pet with compassion, utilizing uplifting feedback methods that regard their feelings and distinction.

2.2 Fitting Preparation to Your Pet's Character:

Comprehend how each pet has its exceptional character and learning style, and figure out how to redo preparing ways to deal with suit their necessities and inclinations.

2.3 Empowering Certainty and Trust:
Figure out how to impart certainty and confidence in your pets, making a climate where they have a good sense of reassurance to investigate and master new abilities.

Segment 3: Reinforcing the Pet-Parent Bond

3.1 Developing the Association:
Find rehearses that fortify the connection among pet and parent, for example, care works out, shared exercises, and undivided attention.

3.2 The Recuperating Force of Touch:
Investigate the remedial advantages of touch in pet consideration, understanding how it supports a feeling of safety and prosperity in our pets.

3.3 Speaking with Instinct:
Embrace your instinct as a pet parent, involving it as an important device to comprehend and meet your pet's close to home and actual requirements.

Segment 4: Past Preparation: Consistent reassurance and Unrestricted Love

4.1 Offering Close to home Help:
Figure out how to be a wellspring of solace and everyday reassurance for your pets, particularly during seasons of pressure or change.

4.2 Observing Unqualified Love:
Praise the strong obligation of genuine love among pet and parent, perceiving the significant effect our pets have on our lives.

End:

Section 6 of "The Pet Whisperer" praises the uncommon association we share with our pets. By speaking with compassion and preparing with heart, we become "Pet Whisperers" who get it, support, and value our shaggy buddies on a significant level. As we leave on this excursion of understanding and love, may we keep on gaining from our pets, embracing the examples of empathy, persistence, and unqualified love they instruct us. Allow us to endeavor to be the pet guardians our darling creatures merit, giving them compassion, warmth, and the magnificence of being heard and perceived. Together, we make a universe of significant association, where our pets flourish, and we experience the unlimited delight of being valid "Pet Whisperers."

Chapter 7
Taming the Wild

In this part, we adventure into the enthralling universe of extraordinary and capricious pets. From reptiles to little well evolved creatures, these interesting buddies bring a feeling of miracle and interest into our lives. As mindful pet people, it is our obligation to figure out their particular necessities and give them a sustaining and enhancing climate.

1.1 Grasping Intriguing Pet Species:
Investigate the assorted universe of colorful pets, including reptiles, creatures of land and water, birds, little vertebrates, and that's only the tip of the iceberg, finding the particular attributes and ways of behaving that make them exceptional.

1.2 Investigating and Planning for Fascinating Pet Possession:
Prior to bringing an intriguing pet into your home, become familiar with the significance of intensive examination, figuring out the consideration necessities, and guaranteeing you are completely ready to address their issues.

1.3 Making a Characteristic Living space:
Investigate the idea of reproducing a characteristic living space for colorful pets, giving a climate that meets their physical and mental requirements for their prosperity.

Segment 2: Nourishment and Medical care for Outlandish Pets

2.1 Extraordinary Dietary Requirements:
Find the particular dietary necessities of various extraordinary pets, from herbivores to carnivores, and figure out how to give a decent and nutritious eating regimen for ideal wellbeing.

2.2 Preventive Medical care:

Comprehend the significance of ordinary wellbeing check-ups, temperature observing, and infection counteraction to guarantee the prosperity of extraordinary pets.

2.3 Taking care of and Communication:
Investigate the accepted procedures for taking care of and communicating with colorful pets, regarding their regular ways of behaving and limiting pressure during human collaborations.

Segment 3: Preparing Methods for Unpredictable Pets

3.1 Advancement and Feeling:
Figure out how to give mental and actual advancement to extraordinary pets, offering exercises that energize normal ways of behaving and forestall weariness.

3.2 Litter Preparing and Essential Orders:
Find preparing methods for little warm blooded creatures and birds, including litter preparing for rodents and showing fundamental orders for birds.

3.3 Conduct Adjustment:
Investigate uplifting feedback procedures to address social difficulties in fascinating pets, encouraging a trusting and helpful relationship.

Area 4: Building Trust and Holding

4.1 The Job of Confidence in Colorful Pet Possession:
Grasp the meaning of building entrust with intriguing pets, as it frames the establishment for an effective and satisfying relationship.

4.2 Holding and Socialization:
Find systems to bond with your intriguing pets, regarding their singular characters and making areas of strength for an association.

4.3 The Delight of Eccentric Pet Nurturing:

Commend the novel delights and awards of really focusing on fascinating pets, appreciating the honor of imparting your life to these phenomenal creatures.

End:

Part 7 of "Subduing Nature" commends the charming universe of extraordinary and flighty pets. By grasping their particular necessities, giving legitimate consideration, and utilizing positive preparation strategies, we can establish a sustaining and satisfying climate for these special friends. As we embrace the delights and difficulties of intriguing pet possession, let us appreciate the miracle and interest they bring into our lives. With adoration and commitment, we can be dependable and merciful pet guardians, guaranteeing that these wild-on a basic level pets flourish in our consideration, and together, we leave on a momentous excursion loaded up with affection and common comprehension."

Chapter 8
Tailored Training

In this section, we perceive the variety among various canine varieties and what their particular qualities mean for their consideration and preparing needs. By understanding variety explicit qualities, we can fit our way to deal with pet consideration and preparing, making an agreeable and effective organization with our canine buddies.

1.1 Investigating Breed-Explicit Qualities:
Find out about the interesting qualities and senses of different canine varieties, from crowding and recovering impulses to monitoring and hunting ways of behaving.

1.2 Comprehension Energy Levels:
Investigate the meaning of energy levels in various varieties, understanding how to meet their activity prerequisites and forestall conduct issues.

1.3 Supporting Variety Explicit Gifts:
Find how to take advantage of and support the normal gifts and capacities of your canine's variety, giving an outlet to their innate characteristics.

Area 2: Customizing Preparing for Individual Pets

2.1 Perceiving Character Contrasts:
Comprehend that each pet is a person with its own character and learning style, permitting you to likewise adjust your preparation methods.

2.2 Encouraging feedback Custom fitted to Characters:
Redo your uplifting feedback preparing way to deal with suit your pet's disposition and inclinations, augmenting preparing adequacy.

2.3 Adjusting to Learning Speed:
Be patient and adaptable with your preparation, perceiving that a few pets might advance rapidly while others demand greater investment and redundancy.

Area 3: High level Preparation and Exercises

3.1 High level Preparation for High-Drive Breeds:
For breeds with high insight and energy levels, investigate progressed preparing methods and exercises to keep their psyches and bodies locked in.

3.2 Canine Games and Exercises:
Find different canine games and exercises that take special care of various varieties' assets and interests, giving physical and mental feeling.

3.3 Consolidating Advancement in Day to day existence:
Figure out how to integrate advancement exercises into your pet's day to day daily practice, keeping them intellectually and genuinely satisfied.

Area 4: The Job of Socialization

4.1 Early Socialization for Pups:
Comprehend the basic significance of early socialization for pups, guaranteeing they develop into composed and sure grown-ups.

4.2 Mingling Grown-up Canines:
Investigate techniques to mingle grown-up canines who might have passed up vital early socialization encounters.

4.3 Dealing with Unfortunate or Receptive Canines:
Find caring ways to deal with assistance unfortunate or receptive canines beat their nerves and fabricate certainty.

End:

Part 8 of "Customized Preparing" praises the variety and independence among our adored pets. By embracing breed-explicit qualities and fitting our preparation to suit each pet's character, we make a positive and compensating preparing experience. As the need might arise of various varieties and characters, let us praise the excellence of our pets' variety. With a fitted way to deal with preparing, we manufacture a rugged bond with our shaggy partners, regarding their extraordinary assets and difficulties. Together, let us keep on supporting their prosperity and guarantee a long period of joy and accomplishment for our dearest pets, embracing the delight of redoing their consideration and preparing for the ideal fit.

Chapter 9
Adopt, Adapt, Adept

In this part, we investigate the special excursion of taking on saved or cover pets and the compensating experience of giving a caring home to creatures out of luck. Embracing a pet accompanies its own arrangement of difficulties and rewards, and understanding the elements of inviting a saved pet into your family is fundamental for a fruitful and satisfying relationship.

1.1 The Awards of Reception:
Commend the significant effect of embracing a safeguarded pet, as you allow them a second opportunity at life, and experience the unparalleled love and devotion they give as a trade off.

1.2 Defeating Difficulties:
Recognize the difficulties that might emerge while taking on a pet with a background marked by injury or disregard, and learn methodologies to assist them with conquering their past and embrace a splendid future.

1.3 Tolerance and Determination:
Comprehend that building trust and trust in a saved pet takes time and exertion, and value the headway made en route.

Segment 2: Making a Place of refuge for Safeguarded Pets

2.1 Laying out Everyday practice and Design:
Find the significance of laying out a reliable everyday practice and giving an organized climate that assists saved pets with having a solid sense of reassurance and settled.

2.2 Places of refuge and Safe places:
Make places of refuge and safe places inside your home, permitting your embraced pet to withdraw while feeling overpowered or restless.

2.3 The Force of Uplifting feedback:
Embrace the viability of uplifting feedback in preparing safeguarded pets, as it fabricates trust and fortifies the connection among pet and parent.

Segment 3: Preparing and Social Recovery

3.1 Fitting Preparation for Safeguarded Pets:
Tweak your preparation way to deal with suit the interesting necessities and awarenesses of your embraced pet, tending to any conduct difficulties with sympathy.

3.2 Defeating Dread and Uneasiness:
Investigate delicate strategies to assist your protected pet with defeating dread and tension, establishing a steady and supporting climate.

3.3 Conduct Restoration:
Comprehend the course of conduct restoration for saved pets, recognizing that each step in the right direction is a triumph worth celebrating.

Segment 4: Commending the Change

4.1 Seeing Development and Progress:
Praise the snapshots of development and progress in your embraced pet's excursion, perceiving the meaning of every achievement.

4.2 The Unqualified Love of Saved Pets:
Value the one of a kind bond that structures between safeguarded pets and their new parents, as they figure out how to trust and cherish once more.

4.3 Showing preemptive kindness:
Investigate potential chances to help creature safe houses and salvage associations, adding to the reason for allowing different pets the opportunity to find adoring permanent spots to live.

End:

Section 9 of "Embrace, Adjust, Capable" commends the lovely excursion of taking on and really focusing on protected and took on pets. By giving affection, tolerance, and understanding, we can change the existences of these extraordinary creatures and establish a cherishing and stable climate they merit. As we embrace the difficulties and delights of taking on a protected pet, let us value the remarkable bond we share with them. Together, we set out on a striking excursion of mending, development, and love, commending the mind blowing change of our took on pets as they become skilled individuals from our families. With appreciation and sympathy, let us keep on giving a protected and cherishing sanctuary for our safeguarded pets, respecting the versatility and faithful love they bring into our lives.

Chapter 10

Beyond Basics

In this section, we investigate the universe of cutting edge pet preparation, taking our preparation abilities higher than ever. By embracing more intricate procedures and difficulties, we fortify the bond with our pets and encourage a more profound comprehension of their ways of behaving and needs.

1.1 Embracing Progressed Preparing Strategies:
Find the advantages of progressing past essential preparation, as we challenge ourselves and our pets to arrive at new degrees of correspondence and collaboration.

1.2 Clicker Preparing and Focusing on:
Investigate clicker preparing and focusing on procedures, giving exact correspondence and refining your pet's reactions to orders and prompts.

1.3 Forming Complex Ways of behaving:
Figure out how to shape complicated ways of behaving, separating them into reachable advances that lead to amazing outcomes.

Area 2: Building Canine Knowledge

2.1 Canine intelligence level Games and Riddles:
Draw in your canine's intellectual capacity with level of intelligence games and riddles, animating their knowledge and advancing critical thinking abilities.

2.2 High level Compliance and Accuracy Work:
Take compliance preparing to a higher level, zeroing in on accuracy and immaculate execution of orders.

2.3 Canine Games and Dexterity Difficulties:

Investigate progressed canine games and dexterity challenges, taking advantage of your canine's physicality and cutthroat soul.

Area 3: Cat Readiness and Enhancement

3.1 Cat Nimbleness Preparing:
Find the universe of cat nimbleness, where felines grandstand their readiness and beauty in impediment courses and difficulties.

3.2 Do-It-Yourself Improvement Exercises:
Figure out how to make Do-It-Yourself improvement exercises for felines, keeping their psyches sharp and bodies dynamic.

3.3 Tackling Cat Knowledge:
Investigate the conceivable outcomes of outfitting cat knowledge through preparing and intelligent play.

Area 4: Pet-Helped Treatment and Administration Creatures

4.1 Preparation for Pet-Helped Treatment:
Find out about preparing methods for pet-helped treatment creatures, who give solace and backing to those out of luck.

4.2 Assistance Creature Preparing:
Comprehend the specific preparation expected for administration creatures, engaging them to help people with inabilities.

4.3 The Effect of Cutting edge Preparing:
Investigate the positive effect of cutting edge preparing on the human-creature bond, encouraging common regard and a more profound close to home association.

End:
Section 10 of "Past Rudiments" commends the excursion of cutting edge pet preparation and the strong bond it manufactures among pet and parent. By provoking ourselves and our pets to arrive at new levels, we establish a climate of trust, understanding,

and shared regard. As we embrace progressed preparing procedures and take part in exercises that animate the two personalities and bodies, let us revel in the delight and satisfaction of seeing our pets flourish. Together, we set out on a noteworthy excursion of development and getting the hang of, praising the brightness of our pets and the significant association we share. With devotion and responsibility, we sustain the human-creature cling to its fullest potential, making a long lasting organization of affection and concordance.